M Helpers

Written by Marilyn Minkoff

Illustrated by Margaret Sanfilippo

Lora and Rick ran into the kitchen.

"Come and sit down," said their mother. "I have some exciting news to tell you."

"What is it, Mom?" asked Lora.

"Please tell us!" said Rick.

"I might be starting a new job soon," said Mom.

"A new job?" said Lora.

Rick repeated his sister's words. "A new job?" he said. Rick looked worried. He wasn't sure he liked that news.

"Yes, a new job," said Mom. "I haven't got it yet. I have to return to talk about it again. Then I'll know if I have the job."

"What's the job?" asked Lora.

Rick repeated his sister's question. "Yeah, Mom, what's the job?" he asked. Rick always liked to know exactly what was going on.

"I can explain while we make supper," said Mom. "The job is at the new museum. I would help set up things. I'd get to work at nine o'clock and return by three, when you get home from school."

"That's good!" said Lora.

Rick repeated her words. "Yeah, that's good," he said. "But Mom, where exactly is this museum? And I'd rather have you work at the pizza shop so we could get free pizzas!"

"Relax," said Mom. "Tomorrow I'll show you exactly where the museum is. We'll explore it together. You two can be my helpers."

"How?" asked Lora.

Rick repeated her question. "Yeah, Mom, how?" he asked. Rick wasn't sure about any of this. But he did begin to relax. Maybe helping his mother explore a new museum wouldn't be so bad.

The next day, Lora and Rick went to the museum with their mother. The first room they explored was the rock room.

Lora picked up rocks and put them on the scale.

Rick climbed up on the large rock. "I'm a rock climber!" he said.

"Excellent!" said their mother as she watched them explore the rocks.

Next they went to the clock room. This room was filled with the sounds of clocks ticking.

Lora opened the door of the big grandfather clock and looked in.

Rick turned the key in another clock. "I'm a clock winder!" he said.

"Excellent," said their mother as she watched them explore the clocks.

TURN ME
UPSIDE DOWN

WIND ME
UP WHEN
I STOP

Next they went to the bug room. This room was filled with different kinds of bugs.

Lora and Rick ran over to see the bees. Rick picked up the honeycomb. "I'm a beekeeper!" he said.

"Excellent," said their mother as she watched them explore the bees.

SPIDERS

"I must talk to the museum people now," said Mom. "They have some things to ask me. Wait here. I'll return very soon."

Lora and Rick looked at the fish while they
waited for their mother to return.

"Do you think Mom will get the job?" asked Lora.

"I hope she does," said Rick. "This place is better
than I expected!"

"You're back!" said Lora.

"What did the museum people ask you?" said Rick.

"They wanted me to report on what children do in a museum," she explained.

"I told them how you explored the rocks, and set the clocks, and picked up the honeycomb. I told them all the things I watched you both do!"

"Will you work here?" asked Lora.

"Yes," said Mom. "I start my new job next week."

"Oh, good!" said Rick. "I'm glad you got it!"

"I'm glad, too," said Mom.

"And you two were my helpers. After watching you explore, I knew exactly what children like to do in a museum."

"You were excellent helpers," said Mom. "Here's your reward. You can return to explore the museum again."

Lora and Rick smiled when they heard that.